DEF
Depression
One Man's Fight to Find Joy

by
Stacy J Brimhall

Soft cover ISBN: 978-0-9969020-6-9
Hard cover ISBN: 978-0-9969020-7-6

Editing: Cecily Markland Condie
Cover design and book layout: Leslie Thompson

Printed in the United States of America

Published by Inglestone Publishing
Litchfield Park, Arizona

ii

Contents

Foreword

In this book, Stacy Brimhall tells his story and that of his family, simply and honestly. Reading *Defeating Depression: One Man's Fight to Find Joy*, you feel as if you are sitting in a room with him, talking casually, but discussing something that is powerfully important.

I was incredibly moved, even compelled, by this book. I have such deep respect and awe for Stacy's strength and incredible mental fortitude in battling all that he has battled. He has faced his demons with courage and ferocity. Yet, his approach is natural, humble and to the point and I find it extremely affecting.

Stacy's book also gave me a huge respect and love for his family—especially his wife and father-in-law—for how they stuck by him and helped pull him through his nightmare.

Defeating Depression is such an important story. It gives sufferers effective tools to help them defeat mental illness. It also is vital for helping family members to 1) understand

what their loved one is going through and 2)
to not forsake those who are living such hells.

I salute Stacy's courage in telling his
story in this way. I recommend *Defeating
Depression* with my full backing and admiration. It will speak to all who read it.

Glenn Close, award-winning actress and activist
Co-founder, BC2M (Bringing Change 2 Mind)

Prologue

When it comes to mental illness, giving up is not an option. It simply can't be. Yes, the pain, the turmoil, the living hell of mental illness is relentless, but don't ever, ever think giving up is an option. This is because, unfortunately, with mental illness, giving up is often synonymous with suicide. And, suicide is not—can never be—the answer.

Yet, every year, over 1,000,000 people commit suicide. That's one every 16.2 minutes of each and every day.

The purpose of this book is to help eliminate—or at least dramatically reduce—this statistic. *Defeating Depression: One Man's Fight to Find Joy* is the story of my own journey in search for meaning and healing through the dark clouds of both situational and genetic depression.

It is my sincere hope that my findings will help others to discover profound beauty and purpose in life, similar to what I have been able to find. Most of all, my desire is that, by sharing my experiences through this book, others will come to the same determined conclusion: Giving up is not an option.

An excerpt from *Defeating Depression: One Man's Fight to Find Joy*:

… an old cowboy … at times, worked for us on our farm during the winter months in Arizona while it was cool weather. In the summer months, however, he would go back to his own ranch in Montana and live. One day, on his ranch in Montana, he was checking fence line. This is a process of riding your horse along the barbed wire fence, checking for any breaks in the fence. Obviously, it's an important job so your cows won't wander off.

One day, while mending a part of the fence, he had a heart attack and fell to the ground. The pain was so excruciating that he just wanted to lay there and die. But, Mr. Leonard had "Fight." He realized that the grass he was laying in was so high that if anyone did drive by on this remote road, they would never see him.

So he had a choice. Lay there and die or prop himself up somehow to where he could be seen if a car came by. Slowly, he started to make his way to the barbed wire fence. It was excruciatingly painful. He finally got his hands on the bottom wire and after about 30 minutes, he was able to climb his way to the fifth wire at the top.

He held on to the top wire, but realized he couldn't hold on for long and would soon drop back down to the ground. So, he slowly turned his back to the barbed wire fence. Somehow he was able to stay erect, and then he wrapped one arm in the wire and then the other arm in the wire as well. His legs then finally gave out on him, and he hung there in the wire in the crucifix position until someone came along and unwrapped him from the fence and got him to the hospital. Mr. Leonard lived.

When I am suffering, I imagine myself climbing the wire. When I finally get to the top, I turn my back to the top wire, wrapping both arms in it, repeating to myself the four mind ingredients of "Fight." Sometimes, my head is down, unable to lift it; yet, I continue repeating the ingredients. Eventually—every time—I finally get the strength to lift my head, give a little smile and wink. Using what I now call The Barbed Wire Principle in this way—and applying the ingredients of "Fight" with tenacity, faith and a willingness to get help—eventually, I am able to unwrap my arms and stand on my own feet.

Philosophy of an Uneducated Man

Have you ever felt anxious or depressed or even angry for no reason at all? The sky is blue, weather awesome, flowers blooming—yet, none of that makes a dent in your sour mood. You have healthy relationships, you like your job, and everything is going great in your life. But, you just can't seem to grasp joy.

For me, it goes something like this:

I wake with a feeling of gloom and immediately begin beating myself up for feeling that way.

I've got to pull out of this. What's wrong with me?

There are dads and moms waking up all around the world today wondering how they are going to feed their families, and here I am depressed and anxious because ... ?

Because my fridge and pantry are full? Because I can't decide what suit I should wear today? Because my closet is too full of clothes? No, wait, because it's not full enough?

What's wrong with me?

I get up, shower, do my daily morning routine and head to work.

Darn, I'm here already. Can't I just wait in the car a minute longer? Okay, it's time ... time to put a smile on my face and pretend for another day.

This may be what many refer to as just a bad day, but what if this is not an isolated incident? What if this happens a few times a month, moving then to a few times a week, and then potentially molding into every day?

For some, depression and anxiety may be situational, the result of the difficulties of youth (being a teenager can be tough), a midlife crisis, a bad hair day, or what their friends or coworkers would describe as, "He's just moody." Whatever the case may be, I believe that at some time every one of us has or will face anxiety or depression related to circumstances in our lives, such as a financial failure, a broken marriage, a wayward child, or death of a loved one.

This kind of situational anxiety or depression can also stem from something small that we normally wouldn't even give a second thought to, but, for some reason, that small thing has turned into a monstrous obstacle. Or, in contrast, situational anxiety and depression can be caused by something more obvious and much more serious, such as by being wronged by someone, sometimes in ways that are even too painful and hideous to mention.

In some instances, the trauma is so severe that it actually damages the brain and nervous system. In such cases, the anxiety and depression is no longer temporary, it's not a "bad day" that will just heal over time on its own. When that fine line is crossed, when depression moves from a temporary situation to an actual change in the brain, or when healing cannot occur on its own, I believe it is safe to say that individual is dealing with a mental health disorder. In others, mental illness may be the result of a brain injury or caused by infection.

Or, mental health disorders can run in families. So, like me, individuals may be born with such disorders in their genetic code and are, therefore, susceptible to developing mental illness themselves.

Whatever the cause—whether situational, injury, or genetic—any form of depression, anxiety or mania can be difficult to deal with at best. I don't in any way want to trivialize what anyone else has experienced, especially in the cases of situational depression. Just as with mental health disorders that are inborn, individuals experiencing the results of trauma in their lives can feel they are in a dark, deep hole that is impossible to escape. They too, are vulnerable, and they too, need coping skills and support in order to escape the darkness. Parents, loved ones and friends should be aware of the fragile state they are in.

Some books I have read on depression, anxiety and other forms of mental health conditions have been wordsmithed in such a way that I tend to get lost. I find they are too "textbook" and not based enough on experience. The author just seems to have diarrhea of the pen. I hope the words I have set forth to write can be a voice from experience and can be helpful and educational, but most of all joyful. Although the subject is not joyful by any means, I hope these words can be words of hope, delivered in such a way as to help bring you back to joy.

I have never been accused of being complex or complicated, but rather one of a simple mind, albeit a mind with a very complex and complicated illness. I hope, in this writing, the simplicity of my thinking will triumph over the complexity of the illness in order to adequately share insights into healing.

I hope what I write will not only be of some help to those who suffer from a mental illness but also those who may be going through or have gone through more temporary, situation-based anxiety and or depression. After all, as mentioned earlier, none of us will escape life without going through some form of sadness, sorrow, anxiety or depression. And yet, these emotions are key to finding joy as none of us will ever truly understand joy without also experiencing these darker emotions.

The main objective of this writing is to try to help the sufferer and those who love and care about them, and so suffer with them. It also is meant to help *all* who read this to develop understanding, patience and clarity in their perception of mental illness, viewing it as they would any of the diseases or ailments from the neck down. Just reading or hearing the phrase "mental illness" in and of itself tends to illicit fear at first. Those who don't understand it often respond to this fear by ostracizing people who have a mental disorder, or even by poking fun at them. Both reactions are equally devastating to the sufferers. Would you ostracize or make fun of a person with cancer? Or, with a broken arm? Or, for that matter, with any physical ailment from the neck down? Of course you wouldn't. Then, why would you shun, laugh at or belittle someone who was sick above the neck?

Please do not feel bad if you have been guilty of such a response. We fear what we don't understand. If your response in the past was to shy away from and demean those who suffer from mental illness, you are not alone. I did it as well. That is, until 1990 anyway.

Mental health disorders come in many different shapes and sizes. For me, it shows up as depression. I believe that no matter what form it takes or how mental illness bares its head, it can lead to debilitation, sorrow, hopelessness and often death.

At the outset of this discussion, it is important to understand not only the deadliness of this disease but also that it is not just those who suffer with mental illness who are dying. Most conclude that if someone has killed themselves then they surely have had a mental illness. Have you ever known someone or heard of someone who seemed perfectly happy and normal (by the way, I greatly dislike that word, for when it comes to us mortals, I believe "normal" has little meaning), and the next thing you know, that person has killed himself or herself? It is probable that that person was a silent sufferer (which will be discussed in more detail later) who hid their mental illness from others until one day they could suffer no more; but there is also a possibility that they were hit by a situation of such great magnitude and speed that, in their desperation of sailing in unknown waters, they hastily concluded that there was no other way out.

For example, when my sister-in-law was in high school, she had an acquaintance whose goal was to go through all four years of high school with straight A's. This fellow student of hers was a happy person who worked diligently to maintain this goal. His senior year, in one of his classes, he unexpectedly got a B+. For me, if I had ever gotten a B+, I would have been doing backflips, throwing a party and having the grade framed to forever hang upon my wall. For him, it was a monumental disaster. He went home from school, closed the garage door, started his parents' car and killed himself. It was roughly three hours from the time he learned of the B+ to his time of death. I did not know this young man or his circumstances, so maybe he had an ongoing mental illness, but also, perhaps he did not. Nonetheless, he is dead!

It could be argued that the young man described above and others like him were "temporarily mentally ill." I don't think it's important to split hairs about that, especially since I believe what I share here can help those who are faced with temporarily overwhelming situations as well as those who have ongoing mental illness that is injury- or genetic-based. Still, my focus is on the latter, as that is what I know and have experienced in my own life.

Many who read my theories and conclusions may scoff. That's okay. In fact, I welcome that! The understanding of mental illness is currently at such an elementary level, I believe the only way we can find cures is to question theory.

Indeed, even though the National Alliance on Mental Illness (NAMI), says one in five adults in the United States experiences a mental health condition every year, and one in twenty lives with a serious mental illness, it seems the definition of mental illness is extremely broad, and the treatment approach seems to be unclear as well.

The NAMI website offers this definition:

> A mental illness is a condition that impacts a person's thinking, feeling or mood and may affect his or her ability to relate to others and function on a daily basis. Each person will have different experiences, even people with the same diagnosis.
>
> A mental health condition isn't the result of one event. Research suggests multiple, interlinking causes. Genetics, environment and lifestyle combine to influence whether someone develops a mental health condition. A stressful job or home life makes some people more susceptible, as do traumatic

life events like being the victim of a crime. Biochemical processes and circuits as well as basic brain structure may play a role too.

The author Andrew Solomon, also a sufferer, said that as he looks back fifty years of how mental illness has been treated, the only word he can think of is "barbaric." He hopes that over the next fifty years, such progress in treatment can be made that we will look back at the treatments of today as barbaric as well.

There are many different reasons for the complexity of this illness and seeming ineffectiveness of the treatment, the least of which is the fact that what medically may work for one affected by the disease, may not work for another, especially as it pertains to medications. That alone may illicit hopelessness to those who have a mental health disorder, as well as those who know or love someone who suffers. So, while I cannot write about what medications may or may not work for you, what I can write about is my own battle with mental illness and what I call the "mind ingredients" that have helped me, and I believe will help you as well, whether you suffer from genetic mental illness or if you are going through situational depression, anxiety, or just a hard time.

Like a medication that has a combination

of ingredients that can help cure or help re-
lieve the pain of an ailment, I also believe the
mind has a combination of ingredients and
that, through rehearsal, exercise, meditation,
prayer and practice, the mind can call up and
disperse these ingredients in order to bring
relief and participation in possibly curing the
illness. These ingredients may not replace the
need for medication and therapy, but may
facilitate healing by preparing the soil of the
mind to embrace the seed and absorb the
life-giving water. For if, as with post-traumat-
ic stress syndrome, there is such a trauma
that it changes the brain from well to ill, then
why can't the brain also be able to change
itself from ill to well? After all, is the brain not
the most powerful and complex organ of our
bodies?

In order for me to communicate my conclusions, I must first tell you my story so you
can understand how I came to these conclusions and theories and then, hopefully, you
can test them against the backdrop of your
own canvas.

Equally important in my story, as well as
in yours perhaps, is that of our predecessors.
Does this illness run in your family history?
Most of us don't know. However, in searching
for answers, we must often look back. Yet,
even as we try to do so, it is often difficult to
unearth all the facts we need. For, if mental illness did exist in the family's past, the

reactions to the illness were most likely to primarily bury it. Hide it.

The attitudes of the past were mostly: "There are no cures. If it ever comes out, they will put you in an asylum and leave you there to rot, bringing shame to the family name."

"Buck up, what's wrong with you? Cowboy up, you big sissy."

"Don't show your weakness. You'll be ostracized, made fun of, called crazy. Any crime or misdeed in your community will automatically be your fault, for it only makes sense it was you, you are 'mentally unstable' after all."

And so on, and so on.

Even in looking back into our own childhoods, we may find some signs of mental disorders. We may remember times of depression or anxiety that may simply have been the result of the everyday difficulties of growing up, or a product of wrongs inflicted upon us by parents, peers, bullies or even our friends. But, whether it's something that seems to be fleeting and situational or if you suffer with a mental illness that has genetic roots and has a more specific name and diagnosis, I again stress that my greatest hope is that the findings in this writing will assist in overcoming outward or hidden torments so that you may find and live in joy.

In my story, there is both the genetic mental illness that ran for decades in my mother's line, but there were also events in my childhood that could arguably have contributed to my mental illness as well. But, whether my challenges—or yours—were caused by one or both, I believe peace can be found; joy can be experienced; love, laughter and forgiveness can occur; and confidence can be restored. The battle can be won—and it can be won time and time again, if necessary.

As I mentioned before, the important thing is not to belabor the cause. What is vital to understand is that none of us gets off this blue ball called earth without experiencing some form of depression, giving us all a taste and at least a little understanding of what mental illness feels like and how fragile the human experience is.

I write this in first person not out of ego or pride, but for two reasons:

1. It is the only way I know how to share with you my story; and,

2. It is important that you understand that this is only one man's journey and experiences.

I may voice my theories and conclusions boldly, as if they come from someone who "knows it all." Please do not interpret them as such, for I am one who knows very little. I'm not a doctor, not a specialist. I share with you my story and conclusions because I hope to be of help to you, but, more importantly, I hope to start dialogue, to have you question my conclusions and dig deeper to find either additional truth in them or to find they are wrong. Either way, it is a win, for the more truth that can be found by uncovering the darkness and uncertainty associated with mental illness, the more enlightenment, beauty and joy to humanity can result. In addition, I believe that through this process, remedies will be discovered for many of our world's social ills.

First Signs and a Beauty Queen

Growing up on a farm, we all had jobs. One of mine was to learn how to run irrigation on our hayfields. By the time I was 11 years old, I was able to run a shift of irrigation myself. A shift ran about eight hours. When we ran water, we had to do it around the clock for two days. My dad and I would switch off shifts during the summer months when there was no school.

My first shift alone, without my dad, was a little nerve-racking. I knew that if I ran the water too long, it would flood the road at the end of the field and possibly cross the street into my elementary school. So, I watched it like a hawk, determined not to make any mistakes.

The system was somewhat antiquated compared to today's irrigation systems that use cement ditches and ports and where opening and closing a port is quite easy. Back then, we had dirt ditches with no ports. So, for each field, I had to dig out a U-shaped trench in the side of the dirt ditch, about two-feet wide, in order to let the water run into the field. Once that field was done, I had to backfill the trench with the shovel to stop the flow of water. I would then move to the next field and repeat. Each field took about two to three hours to complete.

My first time doing it alone didn't exactly go as planned. When the first field was nearly done, I started to backfill the trench. At least I tried, but no matter how quickly I threw in the dirt with the shovel, it would just wash into the field, making no dent in stopping the water. My strength was not sufficient at age 11 to get large enough shovelfuls of dirt to not have it wash away when I threw it in the trench. I became panic stricken.

I knew I had to hurry and figure out what to do. Anxiety ran high, higher than at any other time in my life. I suddenly had an idea. I knelt down into the trench in order to slow down the water with my body and then, with my arms, I took the dirt that sat on each side of the ditch bank and pushed it in front of my legs. It worked. Slowly, I was able to get the trench filled in and the water stopped.

I quickly got up and dug out a trench for the next field to start its irrigation. After that, my body began to shake uncontrollably. Why? The water wasn't cold. As a matter of fact, it felt good to be soaked through on a hot August afternoon in Arizona, so why was

I shaking? I laid down on the ditch bank. Eventually, my body stopped shaking and I was able to go back to work. I couldn't understand what went wrong that caused my body to shake uncontrollably, but once it stopped and I went back to work, I didn't give it much more thought.

In fact, I really didn't think about it again until fourteen years later, when it happened again. This time, the uncontrollable shaking did not stop and my hell began.

In 1988, after some difficult years during my adolescence, I finally started to feel fulfillment and accomplishment, whereas before that, our family was more in survival mode, as will be explained later. That said, until I was 12 years old, I had a pretty normal, if not exceptional, childhood. My mother was an extraordinary mother who made our home a place of refuge and happiness, no matter what difficulties we may be facing; and my dad was always a very loving and caring father and good provider. I loved sports, friends and the feeling of accomplishment after a day's hard work. I know the latter may seem strange for a 12-year-old, but my parents pushed us through the dislike stage of having jobs, to the understanding of happiness that comes from accomplishment and a job well done.

When I was 10, my parents decided

we were going to move from the big city of Tempe, Arizona, to the small farming community of Gilbert, Arizona, population of about 3,500, plus or minus.

We sold our house in Tempe, but my mother only felt it would be appropriate for us to paint the entire interior before leaving, even though the buyer was purchasing the house "as is." So, for five days over the summer, we worked from dawn to dusk, or what we called from "can see" to "can't see," painting our house. I thought I was going to die.

Aren't there some laws against this? I'm only 10.

However, after the fifth day, and having painted the entire house, my mom walked us through the house. It was exquisite, a thing of art and beauty, and I had helped make it that way. The feeling of accomplishment was amazing, it was a feeling I had never felt before.

Once in Gilbert, we actually became small farmers with 50 acres of ground. That was when I really learned to work, even if at times I didn't want to. However, I never felt any sense of accomplishment or confidence in the classroom, like I did with a shovel or paintbrush. In school, I struggled and I spent most of my time in Special Ed classes. As I was learning, or better said, *trying* to learn, to read and write, my teachers found I had a rather severe learning disability called dyslexia. So, off to Special Ed I went, and from then until I graduated from high school, I had spent ten out of twelve years in some form of Special Education classes. I wanted to be a good student. I worked very hard to be a good student, but nonetheless, I just couldn't keep up with the other kids.

By the time I was in 6th grade, I just grew to accept it. That was until, one day on the playground, I saw Angie Dunn, and I was in love! But, Angie was an exceptional student and I knew, when we entered 7th grade, I would never be in any of her classes. I would be resigned to only seeing her during lunch or maybe after school on the walk home. That's when I resolved that, no matter how hard or difficult, by the 7th grade, my time in Special Education classes would be over. I was going to excel to the point that 7th and 8th grade were going to be spent in normal classes and, if I was lucky, some with Angie Dunn! I did it, too.

My dad was overjoyed and my mom said she always knew I could do it. The joy that showed on their faces was almost worth the struggle, but the big payoff was: normal classes, and yes, even one with Angie. Junior high was true bliss. I was able to see Angie both at lunch and during physical education class. I don't know about you, but my first crush was an affair from afar, because I still hadn't developed the courage to talk to her. Still, just being able to see Angie twice a day was enough. I was also happy with the joy and confidence of not only having success with a shovel, but now also finding success with a pen and paper in the classroom.

That joy and confidence started to erode however, when, during the Christmas holidays in 1975, we found out that my mom had cancer and we were told she had only a short time to live. The doctors estimated two years.

Far less important than that, but significant to our detriment, we were not insured. We started selling off everything we could sell in order to pay for my mom's treatment. I would speculate that most 12-year-old boys would not necessarily feel or sense personal responsibility if a financial catastrophe hit their family, but I did.

Soon, we had nothing left to sell and, with that, her treatments stopped.

At the time, there was no public backstop for us. What were we to do? The doctors and hospital floated us for a while, but when our bills got above a certain amount, they could not float us any longer.

We were in a quandary about what to do. Fortunately for us, my uncle found a program study being conducted at Georgetown University in Washington, D.C. After making applications, the university enrolled my mother into the study, which meant they would treat the cancer at no expense to us.

So during the summer of 1978, between my 8th and 9th grade years, we moved to Great Falls, Virginia, a suburb of Washington, D.C.

My sister and I enrolled into Langley High School. Langley was one of the top 10 high schools in the country for academics at the time, and it was estimated then as a whole, Langley was at least two years ahead of the schools of our small farm town of Gilbert, Arizona. Right back to Special Ed I went.

On May 17, 1979, my mother died. I was 15 years old. To this day and forever, I will always have a warm spot in my heart for the people of northern Virginia and Georgetown University for the loving refuge they provided us in the last years of my mother's life.

Shortly after her passing, my father remarried a woman who seemed nice. In short order, my sisters and I learned that she was anything but nice. When my dad was around, which was seldom due to his work schedule and travel, she treated us kindly; but, when he wasn't around, she was abusive to us. It wasn't so much physical abuse, but she was psychologically and emotionally abusive to us. As an example, when my dad would get home, she would pull him aside and tell him fabricated stories of what we did or said to her when he was away. He would get mad at us and would not believe us when we told him she was lying. I started to think that when my mom died, the person I knew as Dad had died also.

Living under these conditions was our new reality. My older sister did so for a year while she finished high school, I endured it for four years and my little sister, eight years.

Once I finally graduated, I was gone. I served a two-year peace mission and when I returned from my mission, I enrolled in a small community college. I wasn't getting any financial help from my father, which made my college schooling difficult. Still, I was determined to get my associate degree. Although a small task for most, it was a large task for me, but I worked hard and finally reached that goal.

At that point, things started to normalize in my life. I was dating the girl (not Angie Dunn) of my dreams who later became my wife. We married in the summer of 1988 and we were in bliss, broke bliss, but nonetheless bliss. I was 24 years old and she was 20. After my mission and during my time in college, I had started a rain gutter cleaning business in McLean, Virginia. I would fly from college back to Virginia for two months in the fall and two months in the spring and clean gutters. This afforded me the luxury of going to school the rest of the year to get my degree.

I had met my wife in Virginia; although, because of the age difference, I was graduating from high school when she was just entering. As I think back on that time now and realize that I was 18 and had a crush on her when she was only 14, it makes me extra protective of my own daughters—a little too protective if you ask them. But, fortunately, this crush was the same as the first; it was an affair from afar, as, once again, I was unable to muster up the courage to even talk to her. It wasn't until four years later that I saw her again. I was at a college football game and there she was on the field, a cheerleader! I pointed her out to my friend who was at the game with me and said, "That's the girl I'm going to marry." It is good to have friends who are honest with you, but once he started to tell me all the reasons that would never happen, the more determined I was that it would, despite the numerous obstacles he delicately outlined. The most obvious of those obstacles included:

- She's drop-dead gorgeous and you're ugly.

- She's a cheerleader with numerous

guys chasing her—guys with bright futures, not a gutter cleaner who, at best, would get an associate degree.

- Her dad is a successful and well-known business leader who served on the Federal Home Loan Bank Board under President Ronald Reagan and who certainly wouldn't allow such a marriage.

- She's smart and you're not.

- Etcetera, etcetera.

Yet, despite these numerous obstacles, I persisted, and to my friend's dismay, she took my call and went on a date with me. After the fifth date, I gloated to my friend that I thought she liked me. Again, he burst my bubble by pointing out that the only time she would go out with me was either on a Tuesday or Wednesday, never a weekend date. He was suggesting she was reserving the weekends for guys she really liked and was only seeing me on weekday dates out of pity or just for a free meal.

But again, I persisted. I decided I would keep asking her out for weekend dates, and if she continued to agree to weekday dates only, I would still not give up until she either asked me to go away or stopped taking my calls.

Finally, after four months, she agreed to a Friday-night date and accepted other weekend dates thereafter. It wasn't until six months of dating that I finally thought I would try to give her a goodnight kiss. I was so nervous that when I finally went in for the kiss, I went too fast and almost broke her tooth. But, although the start of the kiss looked like it was going to be a train wreck, the rest of the kiss was amazing! Not only did she kiss me back, but she *really* kissed me back!

I called my friend and told him, for we had a bet going: If she ever kissed me, he would get on top of the highest building on the university campus, at midnight, naked, and urinate over the edge. It wasn't until a year later, when we got engaged, that he finally did it, or at least he said he did. (That was one thing I didn't want to see.)

It was over Christmas break of 1987 when I requested her dad's permission to ask his daughter to marry me. Although I had never tasted alcohol before, at that point I wished I had a drink just to take the edge off my nerves and to build up my courage. We were at her house watching a movie when her dad stepped out in the back yard to have a cigarette.

A few minutes later, I went outside to talk to him. It was pitch black, with no moon and the only thing I could see was the glow from his cigarette. After asking him the question, there was awkward silence, then he took a long drag on his cigarette that seemed to last an eternity. Whatever confidence I had built up vanished when he finally took the cigarette from his mouth and blew the smoke in my face. He asked me how I was going to support her. I told him about my rain gutter cleaning business. Can you imagine, he being a man who had served on the Federal Home Loan Bank Board of the United States of America and a successful businessman, having some punk kid with little potential and education asking him for his daughter's hand in marriage?

He told me I would have his blessing if she agreed to marry me but if she said no, then I was trespassing and would need to leave. He also told me that there are three types of abuse: physical, mental and spiritual; and if I abused his daughter in any way, then he would pay me a most unpleasant visit. I believe the exact words he used were that he would "take me out."

Mom's Battle

Unbeknownst to her children, my mom suffered from mental illness. How did she hide it from us? What did she do to survive the anguish, pain and torment? As you read on, you will learn of some of her methods that, I believe, will bring you some better understanding of the illness. By far the most important thing that worked for her was this: She unearthed the healing powers of laughter.

As my father reminisces about the wonderful years they had together, some of his fondest memories are of her laughter. He often states that in the short time they had together, she was not only raising us kids but also was raising him. One of the things that brought disappointment to my mom about my dad was that early on in their marriage, she found he would rather spend time with people of influence, rather than his kids. My dad taught religious studies at the University of Idaho and was very enamored with church leaders of his faith and of other faiths and with people of influence and money as well.

On one occasion, he was able to go to a conference to listen to instruction from some of the leaders and professors he admired. Dad was like a kid in a candy store in anticipation of possibly being able to meet some of these men and women, much like a young teenager's excitement to meet their favorite famous musicians. This was something that always bothered my mother; she didn't like that he lacked desire to spend time with his own kids, yet was giddy to spend time with people he thought were influential.

The conference was to be held on a Saturday. My parents arrived on a Friday evening and stayed the night in the same hotel where many of these "influential men and women" would be staying. To the chagrin of my father, that evening he did not see any of them passing in the halls or in the restaurant at the hotel. But, the next morning his fondest dreams were realized. As he and my mom were getting on the elevator that would take them down to the lobby to attend the conference, the doors opened and standing in the elevator were many of the influential people Dad was so eager to meet. My parents got on the elevator and faced the doors, for the elevator was very packed. As my mom held my dad's hand she could feel his hand shaking with anticipation, and she knew, when they exited the elevator he would turn around and introduce himself to each of them, with hopes to walk with them and try to win their attention and good favor all the way to the conference. This disgusted her. As the elevator started to descend toward the lobby, she pushed the button for the second floor. My dad looked at her in surprise, wondering what she was doing. When the doors opened on the second floor, she quickly stepped off the elevator, turned around and said, "Thank you so much, Mr. Brimhall, for such a wonderful and pleasurable night! Please call me when you are once again in town." And then the doors shut.

My dad was in shock, as he looked around at the men and women in the elevator and tried to explain that she was his wife. As you can well imagine, the looks he got told him that they did not believe him and, when the elevator door finally opened at the lobby, they all quickly made their exit, trying their best to avoid eye contact with him.

When he found her later, she was sitting on the hotel step, laughing so hard she was in tears. Even though my dad was mad, he recognized what she was trying to teach him, and his anger quickly faded and he began to laugh as well.

Another method my mother found that helped her was something I discovered from an entry in her journal. She wrote about being busy, regardless of the harrowing, inexplicable sorrow she felt inside. If she kept busy then she would be too busy to have a breakdown. For her, the "busy" couldn't be that of shuffling papers or working on a factory line; she had to be busy serving others. To be meaningful to her, she also had to be serving with at least one of her children working alongside her. As I read this in her journal, a whole burst of memories came rushing through my mind, along with an even greater appreciation and admiration of just how tough she was.

In 1976, even though my mother was suffering greatly at this time from breast cancer, this did not stop her from participating as much as possible with her children. She became my "Scout Mother," or leader of my Boy Scout troop, which consisted of about 10 rambunctious 12- to 14-year-old boys.

In the '70s, Gilbert, Arizona, was a very small town with only one police officer and a small main street. Because most of the workforce in Gilbert was made up of farmers and farmhands, Main Street tended to get quite dusty, with a lot of dirt and mud collecting along the curbs.

On a few occasions, Mom would lead us in doing service of sweeping and cleaning up Main Street. So, on one Wednesday afternoon after school let out, she got some cones and yellow ribbon and closed off Main Street so we could clean it. Unknown to us, Gilbert had recently hired a new police officer, doubling its police force. The new hire was a young man who was very impressed with his newfound authority. As we were cleaning, this officer came up to my mother and proceeded to write her a ticket for closing down Gilbert Road without a permit. She informed the officer that we had cleaned Gilbert Road many times in the past and the sheriff had no problem with us doing it. As a matter of fact, she assured the officer, the sheriff was quite pleased that we provided this service.

This young man was so caught up in the sense of his own power and this wonderful opportunity to write his first ticket, the fact that his boss allowed it in the past made no difference. He was going to see that we were punished for our "offense."

Mom was always slow to anger but once the line was crossed, she held nothing back. After numerous chemotherapy treatments for her cancer, and a radical mastectomy of one of her breasts, not to mention the financial struggles we were having, this officer's attitude was the straw that broke the camel's back. She lost her temper with him and told him that he would immcdiatcly stop writing the ticket and walk away. As you can imagine, all of us Scouts just stood there watching in complete shock as the events unfolded. In the face of her demands, the officer was beside himself and started to pull out his handcuffs to arrest my mom.

This is when the totally unexpected happened. Mom reached down into her shirt and pulled out her prosthetic boob. It was in the shape of a boob but had a thick liquid gel inside and thick plastic sidewalls. The officer, as well as us Scouts were stunned to see this phenomenon, but it paled in comparison to the next event. She took the prosthetic boob, reared back her arm and threw her boob right into the officer's face. It hit him square in the nose and, like most times when someone is hit in the nose, tears welled up in his eyes as his jaw hung down in total shock at what just occurred. His eyes registered complete despair as he looked at us Scouts and a few other bystanders. He shuffled his feet from side to side, having no idea what to do, as this beautiful but angry women was staring him down. Finally, unable to hold up under her gaze any longer, he dropped his ticket book and ran away. My friends and I and other bystanders stood there in shock and silence. Finally, one Scout mustered up the courage and asked, "Mrs. Brimhall, do they all come off like that?"

She began to laugh, releasing the pressure of the situation. Her laughter was contagious, even if some of us Scouts still didn't know if boobs were all removable or not, we were all laughing. She laughed so hard she had to finally sit down on the curb. Her laughter defused the intensity of the situation, bringing us all to a greater love and appreciation for our fearless, boobless leader.

I tell you these stories to not only demonstrate that, for her, laughter and being of service were, if not a remedy, at least a reprieve from her suffering, but also to point out one of my theories about mental illness. I believe that if a person does not get medical help, which in the '70's there really wasn't any, the person is likely to either kill themselves or become a "silent sufferer," quietly hiding the illness as best they can. This latter process of silent suffering, I believe, taxes the body to such a degree that the body often finds a way of taking its own self out, via cancer, heart attack or some other disease. My mother died from having a body littered with cancer, but I believe the cancer was a byproduct of what really killed her, which was silently suffering with mental illness.

But, despite this silent suffering, Mom was determined to live. Even if this silent suffering was going to eventually kill her, she was not going to take her own life; and whatever time she did have, she was going to cherish. She was going to love, laugh and serve. Out of the painful dust of depression, she was going to rise, if only for a short duration. She died at age 39, having lived each day as a lion and seldom a lamb.

Does this mean my mom was a stronger person than those who, seeing little hope for help, take their own lives? Or does it mean she was better than those who openly suffer, seek out help, but then ultimately decide that they can't take it anymore, and it would be best for themselves and all those that love them if they weren't here anymore; so they kill themselves? Or what about the people who suffer, get help but then just seem to exist, as if stuck in quicksand but never going completely under? Was she just a better, stronger, more faithful person than those who have committed suicide or who just exist, living joyless lives? Perhaps it could be argued that she was stronger, but I don't think she would say that. I believe she wouldn't consider herself stronger or better in any way. I believe she would see them as equals with her, each with an illness few can understand, each suffering excruciating pain, which could be argued is a suffering second to none other—for it doesn't end, it doesn't sleep. It continues tick-tock, tick-tock, tick-tocking until something mercifully turns off the clock.

I have heard some people suggest that people who have killed themselves are weak and selfish. Other than criticizing my wife, kids or my horse, I don't believe there are any other words that can be said that bring such insult, to the point of my wanting to lash out, swing and fight. I bite my tongue, knowing they have no clue of what they speak. For,

I believe that most of those who have killed themselves have not been solely motivated by a selfish desire to stop the tick-tock of the clock of their *own* suffering. Having contemplated it myself when deep depression first hit me in 1990, my thinking—unreasonable though it was, but that was reasonable to me at the time—was that I needed to protect those I love and end the suffering that I had been causing them.

Sufferers believe killing themselves would allow their loved ones to move on, to find a better spouse, to allow their kids' mommy to find a daddy who isn't crazy, or to free their parents up to enjoy their other kids without having to worry about their one horrific child. Unreasonable thinking, yes, but in the sufferers' mind it is all very reasonable; the sufferer believes committing suicide would be a selfless act of love for those they care about.

That said, I hope that, through my mom's example, as well as through my experiences you will learn more about as you read on, you will see that killing oneself *is not* the answer. I hope that through my findings, conclusions and theories, the sufferer and those who love them will learn there is another way, an alternative that can heal and provide an avenue to joy; both for the sufferer and those that are suffering with them.

For I believe that with mental illness,

whether genetic or situational, you have choices:

1. You have the choice to silently suffer, which is a silent weeping of internal tears that flood the soul to the point of drowning with no lifejacket, eventually not caring or even wanting a lifejacket, which ultimately leads to either killing oneself or allowing the wave of tears and suffering to find another way of drowning the body.

2. You have the choice to openly suffer, getting help, but just joylessly existing, sinking in quicksand but never going under, only having the tools and giving enough fight to keep one's head above the quicksand, but not enough to get out of it.

3. You have a third choice, which may be the most difficult of all, but, I believe, is the choice that will produce the best long-term results and the most joy. That is to choose to call up the "mind ingredients" to get what I call "Fight." Putting these mind ingredients of "Fight" into practice will require labor, discipline, personal cost, endless exercise—and what I call The Barbed Wire Principle—but, I believe, these ingredients and this powerful principle

will ultimately allow the mind to start mending.

The ingredients of "Fight" will be presented shortly, but first, I share more backdrop of my family so you will be able to more fully understand the ingredients of "Fight" and their purpose.

Dad's Battle: Cowboy Up

So far, in the little I've written about Mom, you have probably gotten a sense that my dad may not have been the greatest of dads: He would rather be with people of influence at the expense of time with his kids. He didn't listen when we begged for him to believe that his second wife was abusing us when he wasn't around. He wouldn't help any of us with our higher education, even though he could have helped since his financial position had gotten at least a little better after my mother's death. However, we learned over time that he loved us very much, but he was dealing with a paralyzing broken heart.

Consider also: What were the circumstances of Dad's own growing up that may have impacted his responses to the trauma of a broken heart and, for purposes of this writing, how he dealt with my mom's mental illness and with mine? And, why is it important for you as the reader to know and understand this? The answer to the latter question is that I believe there are things you can learn from my dad and his responses, giving perspective from eyes of one who is suffering because those he loves the most are suffering. It was all the more difficult for my dad because mental illness is a disease he didn't understand, and, as you will shortly see, a disease that required a response from him that ran totally contrary to his own upbringing.

My dad grew up living the life of a cowboy. You pulled yourself up by your own bootstraps, or you didn't survive. He was born in a rock house in the summer of 1937. He and his twin were the youngest of thirteen kids. Grandpa taught school, had a cow business and ran a freight business as well. The kids were all part of the labor force that allowed the family to make ends meet.

One time, when my dad was 11, during branding season, he was trying to throw a yearling bull in order for grandpa to brand it and cut off its unit to make it into a steer. Whether this bull was observant enough from the experiences he saw of his fellow bulls who went before him that he realized that if he got thrown down, not only was he going to get branded, but even worse, he was going to get his testicles cut off; or if that bull just didn't want to be thrown, we will never know, but in the process, as my dad was trying to throw this bull, the bull stepped on his hand, removing all the flesh between his thumb and his index finger. Grandpa went over and picked up the chunk of flesh out of the dirt and proceeded to wipe it clean in his hands. He then took some of the strong-smelling horse medicine called methylate and dipped my dad's hand in it as well as the chunk of flesh. If you think you've felt sting before when you've gotten a little salt in a cut, this horse methylate would make that little sting seem like a Sunday-go-to-meeting-picnic in comparison.

My dad passed out. When he woke up, he was propped up against the fence with his entire hand wrapped up in black tape. After Grandpa had cleaned the wound and the chunk of flesh, he put the flesh back between the thumb and the index finger and then taped it up. When my dad finally came to again, Grandpa told him to get up and said for him and his brother to "go get that damn bull and let's finish the job;" and they did.

Grandpa and then later, my dad, had been born in the same small cow town of Snowflake, Arizona, located in the northeastern mountain area of the state. Like Dad, Grandpa was also one of the younger boys of a large family. Grandpa learned quickly that the first one up was the best dressed, but unless he quickly got out of the house, his older brothers would tackle him down and take his hat and shoes.

The Snowflake area of Arizona is very

windy and although it is good grazing land for cattle and has good water, it's not an area that has seen much growth like other parts of the state. My great grandpa, as well as my grandpa always told their boys that the only time it would ever be too windy to work is when they put a crowbar through the knothole of the house, and if the crowbar bent backwards, then, and only then, was it too windy to work. Ironically, many of those ranches today are filled with windmills creating green energy for Arizona and good cash flow for the landowners.

On one occasion when he was young, Grandpa was determined to leave the house with the best hat he could find; so, he grabbed the hat and started to hightail it out of the house as fast as his little legs would take him. Of course, he was being chased by his older brothers but, with a substantial lead, he felt comfortable enough to mock them as he ran. His older brothers were yelling at him to get back there, so Grandpa proceeded to yell back, "Finders, keepers, losers, weepers..." The problem was, Grandpa didn't see the rock that was thrown at him as he was yelling back. It was the perfect throw, lodging right into his mouth and taking a few teeth with it. Needless to say, Great Uncle Joe got his hat back and Grandpa had to drink his meals for a few weeks until his mouth healed up.

One more story of the family's "cowboy up" expectations illustrates how my father's background may have affected the way he dealt with a wife and a son with mental illness. My dad's oldest brother was Uncle Kirk. For most of Uncle Kirk's youth, he worked the freighting business. This consisted of fully loading eight to twelve pack mules with trade goods and delivering them throughout the state. Once Uncle Kirk turned 14, Grandpa felt he was man enough to make these trips alone. Grandpa's biggest customer was the Apache Indian Tribe. The Apaches spent the summers near Snowflake, but would travel down to the Phoenix Valley for the winters. They wintered in a place that now is a town affectionately called Apache Junction.

Uncle Kirk died many years ago, but I was fortunate to spend some time with him and learn some of his history. The one question that I failed to ask, but wished I knew more about, was what kind of goods did he trade with the Apaches?

What I did learn was that, on one particular trip, Uncle Kirk was hauling a large mule train down through the Salt River Canyon to Apache Junction and, one night while camping, one of the mules got spooked by something. If you have never seen the Salt River Canyon, it is like the earth stood up on its tippy toes and shook the bottom out of the cookie jar. It's country that stands up on its side. I think only the Grand Canyon trumps the Salt River Canyon.

Uncle Kirk had failed to tie up the mule properly; so, whether it was scared by a mountain lion or bobcat or whatever else, that mule cut loose and jumped right over the edge, riding nothing but air, until an abrupt stop 500 feet down.

To fully understand the gravity of this tragedy, back then the family's mules were probably the greatest buffer between their survival and their starvation. Not only were the mules used for hauling goods but more importantly for plowing and disking the ground in order to grow food. So, the death of this mule was a great loss to the family. How would Uncle Kirk ever explain it to Grandpa? Uncle Kirk had no other choice than, once retrieving whatever he could from the dead mule, to continue on to Apache Junction and deliver the goods.

After the goods were delivered, Uncle Kirk was to load up the mules with the stuff Grandpa had traded for with Chief Eagle and bring it back up the mountain. Uncle Kirk had a few more days in the saddle before he made it to Apache Junction, so he racked his brain to find any way he could soften the blow to the family for the loss of the mule. It finally came to him, he would re-trade the deal with Chief Eagle. He decided although

Grandpa had agreed to trade Chief Eagle two bushels of wheat for ten blankets, Uncle Kirk thought the wheat was really worth twenty blankets, hoping to eventually agree on something like twelve to fifteen blankets. To Uncle Kirk's great surprise, Chief Eagle agreed immediately to whatever Uncle Kirk suggested, without any negotiations. If Uncle Kirk said twenty blankets, twenty blankets it was. The trip back to Snowflake would take anywhere from seven to twelve days, and by the time he had arrived back home, Uncle Kirk knew in his mind that not only was the loss of the mule a blessing in disguise but also that he certainly was a far better business man than his own father.

As they unpacked the mules, Uncle Kirk explained the whole thing to Grandpa, thinking he would be pleased. Grandpa was a man of few words. After the mules were unpacked, Grandpa said to Kirk, "Son, when I shake a man's hand on a deal, that's the deal. We don't re-trade in our family." Grandpa commenced then to tie the re-traded goods back on the mules and, without even being able to stay one night in his own bed, Uncle Kirk had to head back down the mountain to return the goods. When he finally got back to Apache Junction, Chief Eagle said, "I knew you'd be back, Kirk, you Logan Brimhall's son."

Against this backdrop of how my dad grew

up, I can see some of the reasons he raised his kids the way he did. Maybe the idealizing of people of influence was his way of hoping to have influence as well someday and not have to eke out a living through teaching, farming or cow punching. Perhaps he could have this influence and earn enough money to give his kids a better life than he had.

Why didn't he believe us when we told him how his second wife was abusing us? Was it, after being taught lessons like the experience of Uncle Kirk and Chief Eagle, that he just couldn't believe his wife would lie? We will never know, he has never said. But, he has disclosed to us that the biggest regret he has in his life is that of not believing us.

Then, what about not helping any of his children with financial support for their higher education? After all, we all worked through those lean years to support the family together. As he looks back on this, he has admitted he has much regret, but that's just how he thought it was done. His parents never helped him, and he was able to get a master's degree. What we also have learned in more recent years is that Dad, over a period of almost twenty years after my mother's death, paid every nickel we owed to the doctors and hospitals in Arizona. "That's what Brimhalls do," he said, "no matter how long it takes."

So, my dad really loved us, but the

backdrop of his own childhood combined with the endless heartache of my mother's death, left him in a state of paralysis. My conclusion that a part of my dad died when my mom died was incorrect. For, it wasn't long until, when I was in the depths of my suffering, I witnessed his paralysis erode and vanish.

The main thing I hope you as the reader will learn from my dad's example is: You will make mistakes.

Whether you are dealing with those you love who are suffering either from mental illness or situational anxiety/depression, or whether you are the one who is suffering— you will make mistakes in what you expect of yourself or in how you deal with the person you care about.

Later in this writing, I will outline some general suggestions for how you may be able to help the sufferer and how the sufferer and their loved ones both can avoid at least some of the most common mistakes.

What's Happening to Me?

What happened? What on earth did I ever do to be rocked to the very core of hell with no escape, no hope, no light, no God, no future?

Towards the end of 1989, my wife and I were blessed with the most joyful news—my wife was pregnant. As 1989 was coming to a close, all was well. Actually, it was beyond well; life was great! I was out from under the influence of my dad's second wife, I had graduated from college with my associate degree, and my wife only had to do her student teaching in order to graduate with her bachelor's degree. Our rain gutter cleaning business improved as my wife had taken over scheduling, creating greater efficiency, aligning the jobs to be within closer driving distances from each other. I was becoming more efficient in the labor of cleaning the gutters as well. Yet, the greatest of joys was that we were together, a married couple with our first child on the way. Even my father-in-law had started to like me ... a little.

Shortly after the holidays, and I don't remember the exact day, but I do know it was a distinct day, not a gradual descent into sorrow but a wake up one morning, and like a light switch, all was turned off. My eyes were open, but my body shook with tremors of never-ending waves. The only way to slow the tremors was to try to stiffen every joint, requiring such strain that within a short time, I had to resign to the tremors, until I could build up enough strength to once again repeat the process. Fear coursed throughout my entire being.

What is wrong with my body?

Upon that very thought, the answer flooded my consciousness.

It is your mind.

My mind? What's wrong with my mind? Why won't someone turn on that light?

The light was on. I see the light is on.

I see the light but where is the light?

I need to get out of bed, but my body won't move. Where is the joy from the night before and the hope for this brand new day? What is hope now that all is hopeless? Why is all hopeless? What changed while I slept?

Oh God, help me! Where are you, God?

What's happening to me?

I can see my wife holding my face, crying, asking, "What's wrong?" I can only mumble the words, "I don't know." The thoughts continued, unreasonable thoughts but reasonable at the time:

My wife is sick.

Our baby may be dying.

Did I clean the gutter yesterday that the customer paid me for or did I only pretend to clean it and scam the customer? I would never do that! Did I do that?

We are broke, our savings are gone! Where did they go? They were there last night.

What's burning? Is the bed going to burst into flames?

I must abort; I must get up! I must go to work, my customers are counting on me. I am Mr. Reliable, I am Stacy Brimhall, and I am not afraid!

*I **am** afraid.*

I can't rise. Okay, I'll crawl.

Over the edge of the bed I tumbled. I stiffened every joint to slow the endless tremors.

I can crawl! I will crawl!

I can't continue the stiffening of my joints any longer. I am exhausted. I relax my joints and collapse, face down on the floor with unrelenting, spasmodic tremors.

I've seen this before. Where? When? Was this what I had experienced on the ditch bank those many years ago?

But, where else had I seen it?

I suddenly remembered that one Sunday afternoon when I heard a big crash in my mom's bedroom. I ran to her door and opened it. She was on the floor, my dad helping her up. Her body was shaking uncontrollably, but once she saw me, she winked at me and smiled.

Why did she wink at me?

At the time, my dad had told me, "Go out and close the door. Mom will be all right. It's just the cancer."

Oh God, do I have cancer?

I feel my wife trying to lift me off the floor.

I'm going to get up! If I can't stand, I will crawl. When I can see my wife's face, I'm going to wink.

Thus it began. The loss of all hope. I failed everyone. Days turned into weeks. The slippery slope of this glass mountain had no edges, nothing to stop the slide. I was suspended in space, like being in a chair that is tipping over, yet stopped in time, never hitting the floor but continuously falling.

If I could only hit the floor! The fear of falling would end and then the pleasant relief of the physical pain of hitting the floor would begin. Where is that danged floor? Where is the bottom of this glass mountain?

I couldn't work. I had no appetite. We moved into the basement of my in-laws' house. The only routine I could muster was to crawl out of bed each morning, crawl to the shower, sometimes needing my wife to wash my hair and bathe me while I lay on the floor of the shower. I would get dressed and read Louis L'Amour books or other Western novels. During the day, after I couldn't read another sentence, I would crawl or, on good days, walk around the house until I was finally able to sit and read some more ... then repeat.

The weeks turned into a month, nothing changing, sliding further and further down.

Doctors can't find what's wrong. No cancer. My body is healthy and strong. No tumors in my brain.

What can be wrong?

"The only thing it can be, Mrs. Brimhall, is your husband is mentally ill and should be put in a mental hospital."

The next thing I know, I'm lying in a bed in a hospital. They tell me I have been there for three days and they want me to get up and sit at a table and color in a coloring book. I do it.

"Why am I here?" I ask.

The doctor looks at me and says, "It's complicated. We will talk later. Keep coloring."

He leaves, I keep coloring. My dad walks in and sits next to me. I put my head on the table and start to cry. He wraps his arms around me and cries uncontrollably.

"I'm so sorry, son. I'm so sorry, son."

I was expecting him to say, "Son, you need to pull yourself up by your own bootstraps. You need to cowboy up."

Yet, between his sobs, all he said was, "I am so sorry, son."

That night, in the hospital, new light was shed about my mother and her line of family medical history. My wife came in the room, beautiful and pregnant, with tear-filled eyes.

My dad then told us, "Son, your mom's dad left your grandma when your mom was a year old, never to be heard from again until after your mother's death, and then, just to see if he could borrow some money. The reason you never see some of your cousins is because they are in psych wards or nowhere to be found. Son, your mom had it, too."

"What is it, Dad?"

"Mental illness."

"It can't be that, Dad. I've always been Mr. Reliable. It just can't be," I plead.

"She hid it from you kids. She was determined not to abandon you kids like her dad abandoned her. She would not be put away. She would live until it killed her, but she would not kill herself."

I had never understood what Shakespeare meant by, "To be, or not to be." Now I did. Mom chose to be. What would I choose?

Here I was in a mental hospital, with a mixture of blood running through my veins of my mom's family, with definitive genetic mental illness, and of my dad's family, with their "cowboy up," and "your worth is based on what you contribute to the whole" attitudes. Here I was in a hospital, unable to support my family or even do most every day, mundane, simple functions.

"Dad, how did Mom do it?"

He then shared with me a few things:

1. "She did get professional help. Even though barbaric in nature at the time, she still got help."

2. "At the time, there really were no medications that could treat mental illness, other than doping the patient. She refused to be doped."

3. "She realized that, with the immense stress it put on her body, that someday, it would probably kill her, but she would not kill herself."

4. "She was determined to live each day like a lion and not a lamb. Some days she did, and some days she didn't, but she was always able to hide it from her kids."

5. "She would search, ponder, pray, and do whatever it took to find ways that worked for her to release some of the pain, even if that release only lasted a short time; but it would not be by drugs or alcohol. One thing she found that helped was the joy of laughter, laughing out loud, even when there was not much to laugh about."

As I crawled back into my hospital bed

that night, I was determined to beat this thing called mental illness. I would utilize my mother's findings. I would get the best medical help possible. I would find a way to beat it.

But, that determination only lasted a few minutes. While lying in bed, before falling to sleep, I once again had given up. I even hoped that, once I fell asleep, God would mercifully send an angel to come get me and take me to a heavenly home far away from my tormented mind and deteriorating body.

The First Ingredient of Fight: "I Won't Give Up, I Won't Be Beat"

Late that night, I awoke. All was dark, even the hallways where the nurses usually worked were dark. I got out of bed. I was able to walk with only a little shaking.

*Why were there no nurses and no lights on in the hallways? Perhaps God **had** sent an angel to get me. If so, the pain of not being with my wife and unborn son would be excruciating, but it would be so much better for her. She could remarry and, this time, not make such a horrible mistake.*

I walked out into the hall. All was dark and no one was around.

Wait a minute, there is someone, a man sitting in a chair across the hall looking at me, but saying nothing.

He looks a lot like my father-in-law but my father-in-law doesn't like me much, and now, because of my illness and weakness, he

really *doesn't like me.*

I turn and go back to bed. My eyes are shut but I can feel the man's presence in the room. I shut my eyes tighter. The man leans down and whispers in my ear, "I will not give up; I will not be beat."

I open my eyes. It is my father-in-law, but it's not the face of a hard businessman or a protective father. I don't see a look of disappointment or anger, but the face of an angel.

He says it again, "I will not give up; I will not be beat."

"What?"

"Repeat after me: 'I will not give up; I will not be beat.'"

I say it.

"Now, say it again."

I do.

"Now, again."

"Again."

"Again."

God did send me an angel that night. Not an angel to take me from this earthly hell, but to start to teach me the first ingredient of

"Fight" (I will explain later why I call it that).

The first ingredient is: "I will not give up; I will not be beat."

I repeated it continuously every day; yet, once I was out of the hospital, no matter how many times I said it, I didn't believe it.

My father-in-law said that was okay. "Just continue to say it."

So, 1990 continued to be a living hell, but I was determined that, no matter what, I would never go back to the hospital.

I was taking the medications prescribed but as is often the difficulty with medications, it took months to find what worked for me. At first, I didn't understand why. My thought was: *Don't most all medications for conditions from the neck down work for everyone in essentially the same way? Then, why not medications for conditions from the neck up?*

A few days after being released from the hospital, I had set some goals for a daily routine. I figured perhaps I could muster the strength to clean two gutters a day, whereas, previously, on a normal day I could do nine to twelve. Some of the medications I was on greatly decreased the bodily shaking; yet, my wife was concerned about me shaking off a ladder or roof. However, I found that if my body did start to shake, I could lay down on the roof, if I was already up there, or I could find someplace behind some bushes until the shaking stopped.

I was concerned that, in my absence, many of my customers had possibly abandoned our service or switched to a competitor. Much to my surprise, that was not the case. While I had been unable to work, my wife had continued to schedule our customers, and my dad cleaned the gutters.

So, slowly, recovery began, two gutters a day, read Louis L'Amour, walk. Work, read, walk, repeat ... work, read, walk, repeat ...

Push for three gutters today? I'll play it by ear through the day. No, I'm exhausted now after doing two. Tomorrow? We'll see...

I did it! Three gutters today! An enormous accomplishment!

Through each day, each reading, each gutter, each walk, I would repeat in my head, "I will not give up; I will not be beat."

Did I truly believe it yet? No, most of the time I didn't, but that was not what was important right then. What was important is that I continued to say it, continued my daily routine, regardless of however small and limited the accomplishments were.

Was getting out of bed, showering and

dressing any easier than before the hospital? Sometimes yes, sometimes no. But, as my eyes would open in the morning, immediately I would say, "I will not give up, I will not be beat!" Did I believe it? Mostly no; but it did get me to my hands and knees, crawling towards the shower, and sometimes even walking to the shower.

I didn't know it then. In fact, I probably wouldn't have believed it if someone had told me, but I was exercising the first of four mind ingredients that would combine to gradually lead me back to joy.

The Second Ingredient of Fight: "Forgive them ..."

Today is Sunday; no gutters today. For the first time in many, many months, I'm going out in public, but a public of people who I know and care about. I'm going to church. I'm excited to see friends.

I'm excited? I haven't been excited about anything in so, so long. Am I getting better? I feel excitement!

My body still had some small tremors, but they weren't too noticeable. I had lost a lot of weight. Thirty pounds. Thirty pounds I couldn't afford to lose, going from a buck-40 to now a buck-10. My beautiful wife holds my hand as we walk into the church. Some people say hello, but they quickly move away. I see some friends, but they turn away. Stoney Elmore comes and sits by me and my wife.

More people ignore me as one meeting adjourns and we move to another. My excitement has vanished; the first of many experiences of being ostracized has just begun.

Stoney, an old war veteran from World War II leans over and whispers in my ear, "Forgive them, they know not what they do."

And, with that, I was given the second ingredient of "Fight." Again, I didn't know at the time how important that ingredient would be. All I knew is that an old war veteran had reached out to me and, somehow, I held on to what he said, somehow knowing it would mean something to me sometime.

The Third Ingredient of Fight: "Forget them ..."

My son, Joshua, is born, and we are now a family of three. The joy of new birth blossoms, even through the dead flowers of public opinion about the boy's dad.

Why should I care what others think? All that is important is what my wife and this little boy in my arms think.

God, please answer just one prayer. Do whatever you want to me, but please don't let this little boy have what I have! Please spare him this pain, this despair, this hell, this disgrace.

I no longer want to go to church. I don't want to go out anywhere in public, other than to and from each gutter job. What if someone sees me who knows me?

I observe the fleeting stares and then I can't help but notice as the gawkers pretend like they don't see me. I hear the behind-the-back whispers:

"He's crazy."

"He's lost his mind."

"He's a nutcase."

"Why is she still with him? Look at her, now there's a woman! She can have anyone she wants! Maybe she's just helping the nutcase until he stabilizes and then she'll leave him ..."

I silently weep. I've been getting help, and the meds are helping, a little. The physical pain is lessening, the mental anguish persists. Although I'm holding on for dear life upon this glass mountain, at least I have found a foothold. I'm not sliding anymore! I'm finally not sliding. In fact, I'm actually even climbing a little; if only baby steps, I'm climbing.

Oh, God, I'm starting to slide. My friends, those that cared about me, have abandoned me. Even worse, they mock me, make fun of me, convince others that I am truly crazy. It's okay with me if they want to leave me, but why then can't they leave me alone? Why mock, poke fun, whisper behind my back?

"I can't get out of bed today, dear," I tell my wife.

"Can't you roll out and crawl?"

"They all hate me, they think I'm crazy. They think I'm dangerous."

"I don't think you're crazy or dangerous. I love you, your son loves you, your dad and my parents love you. Besides that, what does it matter what anyone else thinks?"

I stay in bed that day. I cry. I weep. I shake. I've lost my foothold, I start sliding down the glass mountain. I once again cry out like I had that night in the hospital, "Please, God, send an angel to come take me away from this weak body and tormented mind."

It's nighttime, but not late, as I awaken from a full day in bed. Fear floods throughout me.

I'm still here. They are going to take me back to the hospital. Please God, not that!

There, by my bedside is my father-in-law. I look at him as he looks at me and he says, "Forget them."

"What?"

"Forget them."

"Who?"

"Those who ostracize you, those who mock you. Those who talk behind your back, call you crazy, insane, useless, dangerous. Forget them!"

There it was, the third ingredient of "Fight"!

He left the room as if angry and, for a moment, time stood still and quiet filled the room. Light flooded into my brain, along with the feeling that I had received another part of a secret code, or another ingredient of an ancient recipe had just been revealed to me.

It didn't quite make sense, as it was a recipe of conflicting ingredients, given to me by different people. And, yet, once these conflicting ingredients were combined, they clearly formed a remedy—perhaps it wasn't the complete cure, but I could see that it was a remedy that could be used to fight the disease and someday, maybe, help find a cure.

I could see the three "mind ingredients" of "Fight" working together:

1. "I will not give up; I will not be beat."

2. "Forgive them, for they know not what they do."

3. "Forget them."

The next morning, after my father-in-law

gave me the ingredient of "Forget them," I was able to get out of bed and walk to the shower.

The idea, and the practice, of not being dissuaded by what other people think finally penetrated my mind and freed my entire being. Never have I felt such freedom, such relief. The line was finally drawn and defined between my "cares" and my "care nots." I cared about what certain people—including my wife, son, dad, father and mother-in-law, sisters, sisters-in-law and those who truly loved me, in spite of the illness—thought of me. Nothing would change in that regard, but the new light of knowledge given to me would change something else dramatically.

I would continue to love those who ostracized me, remembering Stoney's quote, from the Bible, "Forgive them, for they know not what they do." Yet, at the same time, I would "care not" what they thought of me. Stoney's ingredient of "Forgive them," and my father-in-law's ingredient of "Forget them," while seemingly contrary in nature, are beautiful when combined.

What was the backdrop for Stoney and my father-in-law, and what had they gone through to develop their different philosophies? What caused the determination of my father-in-law to never give up, no matter how tough it got? What had occurred in his life to require such determination? Conversely, how

did Stoney, an old soldier, learn about forgiveness? Wasn't war about hate? How could
one live through war without developing
hate? Yet, Stoney was a man who was forced
to kill or be killed, and here he was the one
teaching me about forgiveness.

Thus began a beautiful journey of healing, not only for myself but for my father-in-
law, whose canvas from youth was soiled by
a hideous abuse, previously too painful to
mention; but, like all other feelings that are
buried alive, they had to be unearthed.

This was true for Stoney, too. Stoney's father died when he was in the 6th grade. Upon
his father's death, Stoney, being the oldest
child, had to quit school and help his mother
provide for the family. Stoney's main job was
to plow, plant, water, weed and harvest food
for the family. His machinery consisted of a
shovel, a hoe, a plow and one ornery mule.

By the time World War II started, his
younger brothers were able to take over and
Stoney got drafted into the war. He partici-
pated in the storming of Iwo Jima. He talked
little of what he went through, but, as mentioned earlier, it was kill or be killed, and
Stoney was still here.

Stoney would come over to the house
often and sit with me, sharing stories of his
youth. Often my father-in-law was there as

well, quietly listening along. One night, like a dam that had finally broken, my father-in-law began to tell me and Stoney about his childhood. Quickly, he went from anger to tears as he told us of how his father would come home from work and relentlessly beat him. He told us about how, on many nights, after taking a beating, he would lay in bed hurting and bruised repeating out loud, "I will not give up; I will not be beat."

This revelation gave me new understanding of what he meant by "beat." He was only five years old when the beatings began.

When he was 14, he finally said, "Forget him." He swung back, landing a right hook that rocked his dad to his heels and laid him out upon the living room carpet. My father-in-law stood over his dad and told him if he ever laid another hand on him or his mother, he would kill him. The beatings stopped. Soon after, my father-in-law left home, put himself through college and went on to become a successful businessman and father.

I now knew why, when I asked for his daughter's hand in marriage, he told me about the three types of abuse—physical, mental and spiritual—and told me if I ever abused his daughter in any way, he would "take me out..."

As my father-in-law had told us his story,

Stoney's eyes had filled with tears. Before that, I had never seen Stoney cry. My father-in-law's tears dried, but Stoney's continued as he spoke, "I am so sorry, Steve. I'm so sorry, Steve. You are a hero. You rose above; you defended yourself and your mother. You did what you had to do."

Stoney then said, "My friends and I had to kill, and many of my friends were killed. You did what you had to do and I did what I had to do. Now it's time to forgive."

Somehow, I had the feeling that these ingredients all worked together:

1. "I will not give up: I will not be beat."

2. "Forgive them, they know not what they do."

3. "Forget them."

Yet, the last two, "Forgive them" and "Forget them," seemed at odds with each other and almost too complicated to fully understand and implement.

I have learned that the two are vitally necessary to combine. I have learned that only by including both can I proceed to complete joy. Yet, "Forgive them for they know not what they do," and, "Forget them," are so contrary in meaning that I have had to rely on a mental picture to make sense of it all.

I view the combination of these two as a silver dollar. I call it my "F" coin, with "Forgive them" on one side and "Forget them" on the other. The trick to making the two ingredients work is to not have the coin lay on one side or the other, but to balance the coin on its edge. When it comes to these two ingredients, it's a very delicate balance that requires constant care; for being out of balance, one way or the other, can disrupt the healing powers of these "mind ingredients."

I hope that, as you read my theories of balancing this coin, additional insights will be given to you that I may have missed, thus giving you even greater insight than just my observations on how to find and maintain this balance.

"Forgive them, for they know not what they do," seems to relinquish liability and responsibility from the abuser towards the abused, allowing the abuser to continue the abuse and excusing the abuser because of their ignorance about how their actions affect the abused.

"Forget them" seems to communicate, "I don't care about you; you are dead to me."

So, how can both ingredients co-exist with one not overly dominating the other and be welded together in such a way as to protect the abused, while showing caring towards the abusers? How can you forgive the abuser but also draw the line that says to the abuser, I will also forget you and what you have done. How can you say: "I forgive you, I love you, I care about you, I understand why you have ostracized me and made fun of me because of your lack of understanding of my illness, but let me share with you and educate you of what my illness is and why you need not be afraid. If, after all of that, you still want to ostracize me or make fun of me, that is your choice. I will always continue to love you, but I will no longer let what you say, do or think have any control over me. I will ignore your abuse but not you."

Let me share an experience I had that I hope will communicate what I am trying to say, whereas my feeble words are failing. The experience occurred one day while I was driving down the freeway. Unknown to me, I must have made an error, for a car came roaring up beside me and, with such outrage that one would have thought I had just slapped his mother, the driver looked at me, flipped me off and then sped away.

My first thought was "What did I do?" My next thought was to catch up with him and give him the finger back. I resisted the urge, but still wished for the opportunity. The third thought was where I was making the mistake. What I mean is, I couldn't stop thinking about him, I was letting him control my day.

I was mad. I was so extremely upset. I told my co-workers about the incident and what a jerk this guy was. The mistake I was making is that I was letting this total stranger control me. My third thought should have been to not give the stranger another thought, and thus not relinquish control to him, but keep the control myself.

This ingredient, "Forget them" is to not give the control over to those who hurt you or want to hurt you. By maintaining control, they can't offend you because you won't let them. Your third thought should be to *not* give them another thought.

The Fourth Ingredient of Fight: "Wink—and then Laugh!"

Imagine how I felt when I realized that the fourth ingredient of "Fight" was given to me long ago, long before I knew I had mental illness.

I got the fourth ingredient from my mom.

She taught me to: "Wink—and then Laugh."

That day so many years ago when I went into my parents' room and saw my mom falling to the floor, shaking uncontrollably, and my dad trying to help her up, has branded itself upon my brain forever.

It's not just the shaking that I remember. Even though I have come to understand exactly how that uncontrollable shaking feels, that's not the part of the memory of my mom that is most clear. It's the wink that has indelibly etched itself upon my mind. That wink forms an ever-changing picture of varied meanings, all of which have been monumental to my journey for joy through this awful hell. It's a picture that has spoken far more than a thousand words, a picture that continues to speak.

At the moment it happened, the wink spoke to me, saying, "Don't worry, son; I'll be okay. You run along now." The wink is probably the only thing that got me to shut the door and walk away. As the years continue to pass from one to the next, the wink has continued to speak to me.

When my mother had died, and right before they lowered her into her grave, my dad opened the casket and placed a rose on her body and kissed her forehead. I don't know why, but even though for obvious reasons it did not physically occur, I felt my mom wink at me. It was a feeling that transcended time, that ignored surroundings, and that reached across the chasm of death and again spoke the message to me, "Don't worry, son; I will be okay. Shut the casket, run along now. Taste, hear, feel, love, smell, look, but more importantly see the glorious earth and all it has to offer. Live, Stacy. Live for me … and laugh."

With that wink, a memory of the many times she had me wheel her out to the yard in her wheelchair came to me. She would have me wheel her out under our trees. Each time, she would pick one leaf and gently rub it in her hands, turning it over side to side, telling me to look at the marvelous miracle of this one leaf. Together, we examined the wax-like skin on its front side, which both worked as a shield against burning from too much exposure to the sun but also like a solar panel, absorbing the sun and transporting its energy for the health of its branches, trunk and roots.

She'd tell me about the tree's roots sending nourishment and hydration back up through the trunk and branches to the leaves.

"Look at the back of the leaf, see all the veins, equally spaced, feeding and hydrating the leaf to ultimately provide oxygen to our flesh, our cells, our blood, giving us life! Don't just look at the leaf, Stacy. See it, feel it, breathe it."

Many pass by looking but may not even see the tree, but even if they do, it's just a fleeting thought of a tree. Others may only see a tree, which is glorious, indeed, but I see leaves.

"See the leaves, Stacy, see the leaves! For they provide the unseen miracle of oxygen. Have faith in the unseen, for that is our oxygen. The unseen is what brings the energy, nourishment and growth to body, mind, and, most importantly, our souls. It's how God communicates to us. He communicates unseen to our souls, which I believe is much more powerful than the seen."

Above it all, I believe Mom means for us all to laugh, to laugh in the face of it all. Laughter allows us to rise above anything that tries to tear us down. Mom's wink and her laughter, combined with the other aspects of "Fight" is what ultimately brings joy.

Nature's Presence

Early one morning as I looked out my bed-room window, I noticed hummingbirds playing in the fountain in our yard. It was a scene I had seen many times, but this morning was different. This day I was truly observing them, their carefree flight, the beauty of their colors, the focus they seemed to have on the activity they were engaged in. The thought came to mind that these little creatures were completely free from worry and doubt.

It reminded me of two scriptures from a Sunday school lesson I had heard several years earlier. Both scriptures are from when Jesus Christ spoke to His disciples in what is now known as the Sermon on the Mount. First, from Matthew 6:26:

"Behold the fowls of the air: for they sow not, neither do they reap, nor gather into barns; yet your heavenly Father feedeth them. Are ye not much better than they?"

And second, from Matthew 6:28-29:

"And why take ye thought for raiment? Consider the lilies of the field, how they grow; they toil not, neither do they spin: And yet I say unto you, That even Solomon in all his glory was not arrayed like one of these."

These scriptures emphasize what I witnessed in watching the hummingbirds. I observed these birds and realized with awakening clarity that they were living completely in the present moment, not worried about tomorrow. I decided then and there that nature was my greatest teacher. Nature lives in the present and is completely obedient to the universe. I decided, in that regard, nature would be my guide.

I practiced diligently living in the present, focusing on the four mind ingredients I had gleaned and, in so doing, I started to have memories from my childhood. I realized this is how I lived as a young child, completely present, without worry—with the four mind ingredients at work in nearly every situation. This is why I was so happy as a young child, before adults taught me to worry. I observed how ironic it is that now, as a parent, I was doing the same thing, I was teaching my children how to worry. Rather, shouldn't I let my children remind me about how to live in the present?

As I observe my two-year-old grandson, he is completely present, going about everything he does with joy and without a care in the world. He is always living in the present moment, not concerned about tomorrow or frustrated about what happened yesterday. One may say, "Yes, it's easy for a two-year-old to live in the present. They have someone who worries about tomorrow for them."

That is true. We can't completely forget about tomorrow. But, there is a big difference between planning for tomorrow compared to worrying about tomorrow. Having the four mind ingredients to work on helped me to operate in the present, while still laying the groundwork for tomorrow.

This writing itself is something I have done as a result of looking to the future. I am writing my story in hopes that, going forward, it may help people, especially my posterity. Still, as I write, I have tried to do my best and that has required remaining completely in the present. How effective would this writing truly be if I wasn't able to be present while writing it? I believe this is what Christ was teaching in the two verses above. If we live in the present, plan for what lies ahead, but not obsess or worry about the future or the past, then wc will truly do our best and the universe will make up the difference.

A bird picks a seed from the ground and eats it. Is he not accomplishing two goals in so doing? He is fulfilling his present hunger now and in so doing, giving his body strength for tomorrow.

Defeating Depression Requires "Fight"

So, again, the four mind ingredients are:

1. "I will not give up; I will not be beat."

2. "Forgive them, for they know not what they do."

3. "Forget them."

4. "Wink—and then Laugh."

But, why do I label them "Fight"?

For some of the ingredients, that label makes sense, but, for others, it seems contrary in nature. Perhaps there is a better label. If so, feel free to label it something else that works better for you.

I label it as "Fight" in honor of an old cowboy who, at times, worked for us on our farm during the winter months in Arizona while it was cool weather. In the summer months, however, he would go back to his own ranch in Montana and live. One day, on his ranch in Montana, he was checking fence line. This is a process of riding your horse along the barbed wire fence, checking for any breaks in the fence. Obviously, it's an important job so your cows won't wander off.

One day, while mending a part of the fence, he had a heart attack and fell to the ground. The pain was so excruciating that he just wanted to lay there and die. But, Mr. Leonard had "Fight." He realized that the grass he was laying in was so high, that if anyone did drive by on this remote road, they would never see him.

So, he had a choice. Lay there and die or prop himself up somehow to where he could be seen if a car came by (and thus, demonstrate a willingness to get help). Slowly, he started to make his way to the barbed wire fence. It was excruciatingly painful. He finally got his hands on the bottom wire and after about 30 minutes, he was able to climb his way to the fifth wire at the top.

He held on to the top wire, but realized he couldn't hold on for long and would soon drop back down to the ground. So, he slowly turned his back to the barbed wire fence. Somehow he was able to stay erect, and then he wrapped one arm in the wire and then the other arm in the wire as well. His legs then finally gave out on him, and he hung there in

the wire in the crucifix position until someone came along and unwrapped him from
the fence and got him to the hospital. Mr.
Leonard lived.

When I am suffering, I imagine myself
climbing the wire. When I finally get to the
top, I turn my back to the top wire, wrapping
both arms in it, repeating to myself the four
mind ingredients of "Fight." Sometimes, my
head is down, unable to lift it; yet, I continue
repeating the ingredients. Eventually–every
time—I finally get the strength to lift my
head, give a little smile and wink. Using what
I now call The Barbed Wire Principle in this
way—and applying the ingredients of "Fight"
with tenacity, faith and a willingness to get
help—eventually, I am able to unwrap my
arms and stand on my own feet.

I also imagine, at that point, hearing my
mom's words to me, "Don't worry. You'll be
okay. Run along now."

As I reflect on this and other memories,
I now see not just a wonderful mother who
suffered from mental illness, but also something exquisitely beautiful, and that has led
mc to another conclusion. I believe, for all
sufferers, there is also a part of the brain that
is amplified, magnified and beautiful, seeing things that others don't. Indeed, a mind
with such capacity that it has the potential to change the world. I believe that each

sufferer's beautiful part of his and her mind is different, forming an orchestra of talents that can create music beyond earthly limitations, transcending to music of angels.

Our challenge as sufferers is to first find a foothold upon the glass mountain, work daily to climb, and, in so doing, constantly search for our internal, profoundly unique talent that makes our minds uniquely beautiful. Our challenge is to find and take our own journey towards joy.

Fight for Joy

When I was finally healthy enough and feeling back to my old self, my father-in-law asked me what it was I wanted to do for a living. I thought that was a very strange question.

"I'm a gutter cleaner," I said.

"I know that, but what is your passion?"

It was a question I had not given a lot of thought to but also a question I already knew the answer to. However, the port of entry into the business I was passionate about required so much startup capital that I had not even put it on my "bucket list" of things to do; and, even if I did, I would cross it off my list because it was an impossible dream.

Again he asked, "What is your passion?"

"Land ... I want to go back to Arizona and buy land, farm land, and large chunks of land so that it could be farmed with adequate economies of scale to farm and make a living, land that also is in the path of growth so that someday a builder will come along and buy it at a high price to 'grow houses,' enabling us to go out and buy even bigger farms and ranches."

"Why don't you do it?"

"Isn't it obvious? The gutter business pays well, enough to raise a family, provide shelter and put food on the table, but not to also buy land."

"Your dad told me when you were 12 you raised some calves you had bought with your own money. You raised them and cleaned ditches for other farmers until you had saved up $1,000, and then you took that $1,000 and bought 10 acres."

"Yes, but that was 10 acres in a remote area and not in the path of growth."

"Do you still have it?"

"Yes."

"How much is it worth?"

"$1,000 still."

"Well then, it appears to me you are now educated and ready to start in the land business. You now know the importance of owning land in the path of growth."

There are three things about my brain that I think make up the flip side of the mental illness, the parts that some would consider the unique parts that allow me to function, contribute and, even, to find joy.

One is, I see squares. I see how these squares relate to each other and how growth will occur on them, and why. In Arizona, the land is laid out in squares, a mile by a mile, making up about 640 acres per square mile. For some reason, my mind is quickly able to see what squares will experience growth and which ones won't. Arizona doesn't necessarily grow in growth rings, like many other places; it grows in sporadic jumps, making it difficult to figure out where it is headed next. The reasons for this are too numerous to explain in this writing, but, for whatever reason, my mind has been able to simultaneously sift through all these variables and know what land to buy and not buy.

Another part of my mind is that it can see and act as a contrarian. Let me give you an example.

When I hear the word "never" used in a sentence, like, "Arizona will 'never' go back to the way it was growing before." The word, "never" always triggers my mind to opportunity. If I hear, it will "never" be the same like it was before, I immediately know it is prime time to buy. In contrast, when I hear the word "ever," it also triggers my mind. "This economy is so good, it will last for 'ever.'" That triggers, it's time to sell.

The third part is the part of my mind that simplifies, taking a complex issue and breaking it down to its simplest form.

Thus began the birth of my new business. We moved from the basement of my in-laws' house to Arizona, back to my hometown of Gilbert. We bought a small house for our family—now a family of four, with the birth of our daughter, Alyssa. We continued to travel back and forth to Virginia in the fall and spring to clean gutters, providing us a way to make our house payment, buy groceries, insurance and diapers, etc.

The remainder of the year we would try to find both farm deals to buy and investors to buy them with us. Gutter money was good for covering living expenses, but not much was left to buy land.

At the time, unknown to us, our timing to buy land was both the best of times, but also the worst of times. The country had just gone through a major recession, dubbed the Savings and Loan Crisis, with Arizona being one of the savings and loan epicenters. Land was cheap, very cheap, but still, after our living expenses, we didn't have ample money to buy land of any size that gave it the economy of scales to farm.

So the "best of times" was that the land was cheap. The "worst of times" was that we didn't have any money to buy it and the few people I did talk to who had money, and who I was trying to get to invest with me, wouldn't. The response I would get was, "Why on earth do you want to buy land? It's toxic, stay away from it. Things will 'never' get back to the way they were again."

They did have a point, but, I realized that most of the resistance was because I was the guy with the mental illness.

My father-in-law introduced me to two men from Holland who had a lot of money, and, based on my father-in-law's reputation, were willing to invest it with my wife and me. As I mentioned before, the timing was perfect. After being able to buy many farms and ranches in the path of growth, the economy started to increase dramatically. Land went from "toxic" to the "belle of the ball." My wife and I no longer needed to clean gutters.

I tell you this not to brag, for having mental illness doesn't allow one the luxury of too much ego. I tell you this only because I believe if you implement the mind ingredients of "Fight," over time you will also be able to unearth and implement the uniquely beautiful parts of your mind. Whether the beautiful part of your mind is something that can bring you money, it doesn't matter. What matters is the fact that tapping in to those areas of your mind will bring you joy!

"What's Wrong?"

"What went wrong?" is a common question I get asked a lot from those who are dealing with loved ones who are suffering from mental illness.

"It doesn't make sense to me, please put it into words I can understand."

"What's wrong with them?"

When I'm asked this, I then proceed into my analogies of "sliding down a glass mountain" or "tipping over in a chair that never hits the floor but is always in a state of falling." For most, those analogies still don't come close to giving them the full breadth of the despair, the suffering or the deadliness of the disease.

Before I try to better describe how it feels, I think it is important for the reader to understand how best to approach, talk with and communicate with the sufferer before they can ever begin to understand how and what they are feeling. Asking the sufferer,

"What's wrong with you?" only creates distance between you and the sufferer, not understanding.

For most people, as mentioned earlier in this writing, it is far easier to understand and be sympathetic and patient with those who have an ailment from the neck down, such as cancer, heart attack, blood disease, broken leg, etc. With ailments from the neck down, the typical question to the sufferer is, "How do you feel?" Or, "How does it feel?"

With ailments from the neck up, the typical question is, "What's wrong?" Or even worse, "What's wrong with you?"

One time, when my son made an unwise choice and did something that was really stupid, I angrily asked him, "What's wrong with you?" Instead, the question should have been, "What were you thinking?" The first question of "What's wrong with you?" implied that there was something truly amiss with him, that his action was not only stupid, but that he was stupid. Whereas, "What were you thinking?" would have implied that I thought what he did was foolish, but not that he had something permanently wrong with him.

Asking a sufferer, "What's wrong with you?" is a question not only about what's wrong with your body but also your person, your identity, your soul. Worst of all, it implies that it is somehow the sufferer's fault, that it's something of their own doing, their own making. Whereas, asking, "How does it feel?" implies, "What's wrong with your body?" This is a sympathetic question rather than a condemning question.

Would you ask a person who had a heart attack, "Why did you allow yourself to have a heart attack, you big idiot?"

After my father's heart attack, I asked him how it felt. He said it was an enormous pressure in his chest, like an elephant was standing on it. With that analogy, I could catch a glimpse of what it may have felt like, but in no way could I fully understand it.

So, even though I couldn't fully understand the pain that was going on inside his chest, I did understand that it was real, deadly and of no fault of his own. Like a heart attack, mental illness is real, deadly and as mentioned before, no fault of the sufferer.

One question to truly ask yourself is, "How would you feel towards someone who has been in the cardio section of the hospital for heart failure compared to someone who has been in the mental ward of a hospital for a mental illness?" If you feel differently towards the two, you may need to ask yourself, "What's wrong with me?"

With that said, I will now try to better describe how it feels.

How Does It Feel?

One evening in the desert, I observed a magnificent hawk sitting solitaire atop a majestic saguaro cactus, a cactus that has stood as a sentinel for over 200 years, for it was well over 20 feet tall. The saguaro cactus not only had seen two centuries worth of exquisitely beautiful desert sunsets (as was now taking place), but also was fulfilling its role with profound clarity as the sun's colors changed upon its thorny green surface. Soon, the colors would settle to just one, as the sun would fade and the lone outline of the saguaro would darkly stand out against the starlit, moonless night.

Amongst all this beauty, there was also taking place the harsh realities of Mother Nature. Although the hawk seemed to enjoy the beauty of the sunset as much as I, his enjoyment was for far different reasons. The desert was once again coming alive with the setting of the sun, as the birds and animals were making their way out of dens and nests to hydrate, feed and explore after a long day of heat. I closed my eyes in an attempt to discern different desert sounds, wondering which one was of most interest to the hawk. I knew the hawk would dine well this night, for there were many sounds to choose from!

Upon opening my eyes, I saw the hawk swoop from its lofty perch. Being desert-born myself, I knew this was not a test flight. Soon, one of the desert sounds would change from a quiet communion to a painful panic, then physical pain and then the last, the death throes as the hawk's claws would penetrate and squeeze the life out of its chosen prey.

With what fleeting light was remaining, I was able to see the hawk once again. Now it was flying upwards with the night's meal, chosen from its large menu, a desert squirrel clutched in its death claws, the sounds of pain squealing from the squirrel's little body, yet mercifully, only a few seconds later, quieting into the soundlessness of death.

The question most commonly asked of me by non-sufferers of mental illness is, "What does it feel like?" I share my analogy of the desert squirrel in an attempt to help them understand. For the non-sufferer, it is a beautiful sunset, but to the sufferer, there is no beauty when depression sets in. There is only the desperate feeling of a desert squirrel being crushed emotionally, physically and mentally by the hawk. Nor is there hope for the mercy that comes from death...unless...

When I see that my feeble analogy doesn't make much of a dent into their understanding, I then start using words like hopelessness, anxiety, alone, confused, exhausted, helpless, worthless, terrified, sleepless, lifeless and empty.

"Why?" is often the next question they ask, followed with, "I don't get it, it doesn't make sense to me ..."

That is when I realize, thankfully, they can't understand it for they have not felt it. They can't understand mental illness any more than I could understand the pain of a broken bone unless I had broken a bone before.

At this confused intersection between the sufferer and non-sufferer is where I believe the most damage occurs. For an illness from the neck down is met with compassion, sympathy and love. Yet, illness from the neck up, is met with fear, trepidation and, ultimately, the sufferer is stigmatized with their scarlet letter and ostracized. The stigma associated with mental illness reinforces to the sufferer that they are useless, worthless, hopeless and inevitably, alone.

So the struggle continues, the fight for inner peace will always be. My choices are the same: kill myself or, silently suffer until my body finds its own way of killing itself or, I can get help. Yet, in addition to getting help, I know I must always continue to fight.

"I will not give up, I will not be beat," I repeat to myself. I must also "Forgive them, for they no not what they do." And, I must make myself not care what those that ostracize me think—"Forget them."

Finally, I must "Wink—and then Laugh."

Getting help is to exist but getting help combined with a will to "Fight," regardless of how feeble the fight in me is, is what gives me hope. This small seed of hope sprouts to greater hope and this greater hope sprouts to joy. So, knock me down, and I will muster the mind ingredients of "Fight" and I will get up.

Repeat if you must, I will get up.

Give me this mountain and, by God, I will climb.

Having felt the pains of mental illness, I have a greater understanding of joy. Having been given the mind ingredients of "Fight," I have the means of hanging on and finding my way to that glorious resolution.

> *"It is never easy to face hardship, suffering, pain, and torture. It is always easier to die, simply*

to give up, to surrender and let the pain die with you. To fight is to keep pain alive, even to intensify it. And this requires a kind of courage for which I had only admiration."

~ Louis L'Amour

The fight for joy continues ...